Barb —
You ...
a 8...
... y
Margie

One of the best feelings
in the whole world
comes from being a friend...
and having a friend in return.

———————
Lorrie Westfall

We wish to thank Susan Polis Schutz for permission to reprint the following poem that appears in this publication: "Our Friendship Will Remain Constant." Copyright © 1985 by Stephen Schutz and Susan Polis Schutz. All rights reserved.

ACKNOWLEDGMENTS appear on page 48.

Certain trademarks are used under license.

Manufactured in the United States of America.

✪ This book is printed on recycled paper.

SPS Studios, Inc.

P.O. Box 4549, Boulder, Colorado 80306

Good Friends Come Along Once in a Lifetime

A Blue Mountain Arts® Collection
on All the Wonderful Things
Friendship Brings to Life

Edited by Gary Morris

Blue Mountain Press™

SPS Studios, Inc., Boulder, Colorado

Rare People

There are rare people in this world
who are so caring —
　　whose natural instinct is to put
　　someone else's needs
　　ahead of their own;
who offer encouragement
　　when it is needed;
who are always there to listen
　　with a smile and a loving,
　　open heart.

There are rare people
　　who never want or expect
　　praise for their good deeds
　　because that's just
　　the way they are.

You are one of
those rare people...

How fortunate I am
that you are my friend!

Andrea L. Hines

Friends like You
Come Along
Once in a Lifetime...

And I want you to know how glad I am that you came along in mine. Friends like you are so valuable and so rare. You provide me with things that can't compare with any other happiness in my life. I am so thankful for all the wonderful things about you. You understand my difficulties and always give me the benefit of the doubt. There are so many times when you're the only one who knows what I'm going through. You're what communication and trust are all about.

If you sense that I'm hurting, you do whatever you can to help me. And you don't hold things against me. You help me prop up my courage if it starts to fade, and you have such a gentle way of providing reassurance.

You walk beside me when I could use a little guidance and direction in my life. And, more than anyone else, you support me in my attempts to do what is right.

You multiply my smiles and you constantly add to my favorite memories. You make me feel like I really am somebody who matters. Then you quietly prove to me how beautiful that feeling is. You really are amazing. And I wish I had a way to thank you for all this.

I feel like it's important to let you know that, in you, I have come across a wonderful, once-in-a-lifetime friend. The gift of that friendship is the nicest thing anyone could ever give... and I will cherish it all the days of my life and all the years that I live.

Emilia Larson

You Deserve
a Perfect Gift

I tried to think of something
I could give you
that would signify all you mean to me.
It had to be something very special
because that's what you are.
It had to be something that would last,
just as our friendship has
    all these years.
So I took all my memories of us
and I added the laughter,
the secrets, and the comforting and
    encouraging words we've shared,
then stirred them all together.
I sprinkled it with faith,
    mixed in a promise of forever,
        and sealed it with love.
Because all along I knew
    that there is no greater gift
than the wonderful friendship we share,
and all I can ever hope to do
    is give it back to you.

Barbara Cage

"Thank You"
Just Doesn't Seem
like Enough

Two words. Eight letters.
"Thank you" just doesn't seem like
    enough to express my gratitude
    for all you've done.
It doesn't seem like enough to say,
    "What would I do without you?"
    It doesn't seem like enough of an
    exchange for all you've given me.
But that's the most amazing part...
    you give of yourself, expecting
    nothing in return.
I wish there were words to express
    how much I appreciate all you've
    done — how much I appreciate you.
But there are no words, except two
    small ones that come directly from
    my heart... thank you!

—————————
Donna Gephart

My Definition of a
Good Friend
Is You

Good friends aren't picky and delicate,
and their friendship is not easily broken.
They don't have to be handled with kid
gloves or tiptoed around. They are tough
and trusting and loyal to each other. They
want the best for each other. They do
things for each other. They are easy and
comfortable to be with. When they're not
around, we miss them and our world seems
out of balance. They are the kind of friends
who stand by each other no matter what.
When they say they mean forever, they
really do.

Good friends have no need to question each other's motives. They know that they're on each other's side, not in competition with each other, and they would never do the other any harm. They wouldn't hurt each other's feelings for anything and they would go to great lengths to protect their friendship because they know it's so special.

There are many ways to define a good friend, but I will cut it short by just saying that... my definition of a good friend is you.

———————————

Donna Fargo

The First Time I Met You,
I Knew We Would Be Friends

We connected immediately with mutual interests and easy, natural conversations. When we're together, I feel relaxed and comfortable. I am more myself with you than I am with anyone else I know.

I love how we laugh and have fun together. We never run out of things to talk about. I confide in you with complete faith and trust. Your friendship has brought a new sense of peace and equanimity into my life. It has allowed me to examine my own life and graciously taught me how to be gentler with the person I am.

Your friendship has brought me a newfound sense of confidence and self-worth. It has given me a special love that remains loyal and true. As a friend, you've given me a piece of your heart. I am fortunate to be blessed with the wonderful experiences we've had. I am deeply honored to have you as my friend.

————————

debbie burton-peddle

As the Years Pass By...

It is easier to see
who the special people are in my life.
It's easier to realize what is important,
what matters, who matters.
Please know, my friend,
that you are very important
and you matter so very much to me.
As I journey along the path of my life,
sharing some steps
along the way with you,
I am touched by your kindness,
I am warmed by your caring,
and I am blessed by your friendship.

Today and every day,
you deserve to be touched
with the treasures of life's precious gifts;
you deserve to be blessed
with the goodness of friends,
the generosity of love,
and graces from God.
May all your days be as special
as you are.

Denise Johnston

A Friend
Is One of Life's
Most Beautiful Gifts

A friend is a person you can trust,
who won't turn away from you;
a friend will be there
when you really need someone,
and will come to you
when they need help.
A friend will listen to you
even when they don't understand
or agree with your feelings;
a friend will never try to change you,
but appreciates you for who you are.
A friend doesn't expect too much
or give too little;
a friend is someone you can share
dreams, hopes, and feelings with.
A friend is a person you can think of
and suddenly smile;
a friend doesn't have to be told
that they are special,
because they know you feel that way.

A friend will accept your attitudes,
ideas, and emotions,
even when their own are different,
and will hold your hand when you're scared.
A friend will be honest with you
even when it might hurt,
and will forgive you
for the mistakes you make.
A friend can never disappoint you,
and will support you
and share in your glory.
A friend shares responsibility
when you have doubts.
A friend always remembers
the little things you've done,
the times you've shared,
and the talks you've had.
A friend will bend over backwards
to help you pick up the pieces
when your world falls apart.
A friend is one of life's
most beautiful gifts.

— Luann Auciello

I Celebrate
Our Friendship
Every Day

You are the type of friend that
people search endlessly for —
a person so caring and kind
so honest and understanding

You are a person who finds the right words
and whose silence is so comforting
when there are none
You are the one person
who has never let me down
the one I run to first when something
exciting happens in my day
the one who carries the umbrella
when life's storm clouds blow in

You have made such a difference
every day of my life
making the tough decisions
a little bit easier
and the wonderful times
so much more memorable

Together we've laughed harder
and talked about our dreams
We've pushed each other to strive
for the very best
and padded each fall
with reassurance and understanding

In our lives we will share many gifts
with many people
but I want you to know
that our friendship is a gift
I am thankful for every day of my life

———————
Elle Mastro

You've Planted
Some Beautiful Seeds
in the Garden of My Life

In the garden of life,
seed-planters are people
who cultivate and nurture others.
Seed-planters sow seeds
    of faith and encouragement
and they always believe
    the best in you.

You have been a seed-planter
    in my life.
With your tender care,
    I have blossomed —
and my heart is forever thankful
    for you.

— Autumn Banks

I Keep Our Memories Tucked Within My Heart

Inside my heart
there is this little place
It keeps me warm
It keeps me sane
It is my sunshine on
    rainy days

This is the place where
I've stored away
each memory we have shared
and all the wonderful thoughts
    I think of you

So no matter where you are
or how far away I go
I will keep you close to me
and my heart will be filled
    with happiness always

Deana Marino

The Friendship Wish

With the rising of the sun each morning, I wish you beauty and a day filled with wonder and promise. At night, as the sun slides peacefully into her cradle, I wish you contentment and the knowledge that you have lived the day, not simply survived it. And in between, I wish you all this...

A heart filled with joy by small and wondrous things — the sweet song of a bird; the ringing, gleeful sound of a child's laughter; or even just a memory that puts a smile in your step.

A life filled with passion. Indulge in lingering kisses and spontaneous hugs. Use strong language; get angry at injustice. Raise your voice, snort with laughter; don't be afraid to be seen or heard, for you are worth noticing.

The courage to face all that life has to offer: the good, the bad, and the boring in-between. Imagine beyond your limits, whatever they may be, and never be stifled by ignorance.

The wisdom to heed the beat of your own heart. This is your dance — you set the tempo. Why line dance when you can rumba?

Mostly, though, I wish you love. Contrary to what some people might say or think, I believe it is okay to go around loving everything — trees, cats, flowers, cars, birds, songs, hats, husbands, kids, furniture, parents, clouds, rainbows, brothers, sisters, fish, sitcoms, paintings, jellybeans, flannel pajamas, chocolate, coffee, cinnamon tea — because all these things make up the life you live.

Let yourself love whatever you wish, my friend, and all my wishes for you will come true.

Kathy Larson

You and I Are Bigger than Any of Our Differences

We are different people,
   you and I.
We have different interests,
   opinions, ideas,
and ways of doing things.
Sometimes, these differences
lead to friction between us.
Those times can be frustrating,
   uncomfortable, and discouraging...
but they don't detract from
the important place you have in my life.
You have so many qualities
   I admire and appreciate.
I value your insight and advice;
I respect your knowledge and wisdom.
So though our differences may seem
   to push us apart...
always remember there is
   so much more
      that pulls us together.

Carrie Cramer

Our Friendship Will Remain Constant

Sometimes we do not feel like we want to feel
Sometimes we do not achieve what we want
  to achieve
Sometimes things that happen do not make sense
Sometimes life leads us in directions that are
beyond our control
It is at these times, most of all
that we need someone
who will quietly understand us
and be there to support us
I want you to know, my friend
that I am here for you
in every way
and remember that though
circumstances in our lives change
our friendship will always remain constant
and remember that though
things may be difficult now
tomorrow is a new day

Susan Polis Schutz

Old Friends Are
the Best Gifts
in Life

Old friendship is companionship
    turned golden;
it takes on a luster like ivory
where love's light has lingered.
Old friends are threads of gold
    in the tapestry of our lives.
They hold things together,
    keep us connected,
and help our world make sense.
Old friends know where we've been,
    where we are,
and where we want to go.
They encourage us to dream,
    and if those dreams fall apart
they're the ones who stay
    and help us pick up the pieces.
They help us build our lives
    better and stronger.

With their unconditional caring,
    they give us the courage
to endure the hard times.
They show us what is best
    and beautiful in ourselves,
and they are gentle and quiet
    with our faults.
An old friend is a kindred spirit,
    confidant, and companion
        in life's journey;
the one person we utterly trust,
    who knows us totally as we are.
When all else has come and gone
    in our lives,
old friends remain.
They are friends for life —
    like you and me.

Vickie M. Worsham

Friendship Is...

...creating a sunny day together, even if it is pouring rain outside.

...making time for each other no matter how busy life gets.

...standing up for one another when challenges and confrontations come along.

...dropping everything when the other person is in need.

...loving each other unconditionally.

...dreaming, planning, and believing together.

...laughing until you can hardly breathe — and not caring who hears you.

...sharing cherished memories and priceless moments that will last for a lifetime.

———————

Jane Andrews

We Go Together Like...

Cookies and milk
candles and birthday cake
ghost stories and campfires

We go together like...
pillow fights and laughter
blush and mascara
sleepovers and truth-or-dare

We go together like...
music and dancing
pictures and frames
popcorn and movies

We go together like...
winter and snow
spring and cherry blossoms
stars and the night

We go together like...
best friends

Dallas Woodburn

You've Made a
Difference in My Life

Sometimes it's easy to think that because we're not famous, maybe we're not important.

I want you to know that you don't need to be a movie star, a bestselling author, an inventor, a millionaire, or anything other than the special person you are to be a hero to me.

I hope you know how much you mean to me and what an important part you play in my life. When I look back through the years, it's easy to see that you've always been there to support me and to tell me that I could accomplish anything I could imagine.

You've laughed with me, cried with me, and dreamed my dreams with me.

I just wanted to take this moment to tell you that all you are and all that you've done for me have not gone unnoticed.

I don't know how I would have made it through the hard times without you to lean on... and the good times could never have been as good without you to share them with me.

If you ever wonder whether you've made a contribution in this life, know that you've made a beautiful, wonderful difference in my world.

Jason Blume

A Friendship Flower

You would think
that we might have
forgotten each other
by now; life is so
uncertain — so many
people come and go,
like rain. But no
matter where I have
stood, or what
roads I've been
down, you have
been there for
me — at every turn
along the way...

...and I guess
that some things
change and other
things don't
and there are
some special
types of
friendships that
grow and yet stay
the same. And
I'm just really
glad we've got
that special sort
of friendship... that
is there for you,
there for you
always.
Thanks for being a friend.

— Ashley Rice

You're Appreciated
for Everything
You Are

I have the sweet and special privilege of
being your friend. And I know how wonderful
you are... in every facet of your life. One of
the most beautiful aspects of all is knowing
what an incredible person you are.

You always go out of your way to do so many
things for others. You never hesitate to take
time out of your life to make other lives
shine brighter.

You have a heart of pure gold, and you just
seem to know what is needed and how best to
help. It is so natural for you to share the
treasure of all that you are,
so unselfishly...

You do the things you do in the most
admirable way of all... from a heart that
loves so much and that only wants what's
best for everyone.

And I know that you could hear it every
day and still never get to hear — nearly
often enough — all the thanks you deserve.

I'd like to be among those who hope you
will remember your whole life through
that you are appreciated so much
for all that you are
and for everything
that you do.

—————————
R. L. Keith

Thanks for Being
So Special

Every once in a while
you meet a special person
who helps you through
the rough spots
and makes you laugh
and understands the words
you make up
when you are stressed
or running at a million miles
    an hour.

Every once in a while,
you meet a special friend
like that...
who makes you remember
things like crayons and rainbows
and good days...
And suddenly everything
seems possible again.

Thanks for being that friend.

—Ashley Rice

Friends like You
Make the World
a Better Place

Friends are the joys
that make us more like family
and the moments that show us
we still live in a caring world.

Friends are the added strength we need
to face what life may bring;
they are always close at hand,
bringing hope to the soul.
They have arms full of caring;
they are there to soften every hurt.
They are thoughts and feelings shared
    but never labeled.
Friends are candles lit by one another;
they are the glow of time and memory
to warm our hearts.

— Linda E. Knight

A Best Friend...
Is What You'll
Always Be to Me

A best friend...
one who walks the extra mile with you —
   a smile-maker, hope-giver,
         heart-warmer, and hand-holder.

A best friend...
one who concentrates on your
   emotional well-being
by bringing to light past victories,
keeping you focused on the positive,
and reminding you that you're not alone;
one who will not rest until
   you see life's brighter side.

A best friend...
one who reminds you it's just a few
    more steps to the finish line
        and you can't stop now.

A best friend...
one who cares so much that it shows
each time you need
    a voice of inspiration,
        an arm around your shoulder,
    and the presence of someone
        who cares completely about you.

A best friend...
that's what you are to me
and what I'll always be to you.

———————
Barbara J. Hall

Friends Are
the Heartstrings of Life

Friends are such an important part
of life, and whether we see them
all the time or not, they are crucial
in the way we see and interact with
    the world.
Friends remind us that the sun is shining,
even though it might be hidden
behind some very threatening,
    dark clouds.
Friends stand by us and are there
to help through challenges,
illnesses, heartaches, and
all sorts of worries and decisions.
Friends keep us from losing our minds,
our faith, and sometimes
our spouses or our keys.

Friends play different roles, but
each one is important.
Some are the shoppers,
others the phone talkers,
some know just what to say
    when there's a tragedy,
and others make us laugh.
The one thing they all have in common
is that they bring camaraderie,
contentment, security, and joy
into our lives.

I'm so glad we're friends.
I feel very lucky to be part of your life...
and especially grateful
    that you are part of mine.

————————————
Barbara Cage

Our Friendship
Is a Promise

Although we may not say it to each
　　other or even realize it, our friendship
　　is a promise.
It's a promise to always be there for the
　　other person — no matter what.
It's a promise to share bits and pieces of
　　our lives with each other.
It's a promise to care so much about the
　　other person that one's laughter belongs
　　to the other, as do one's tears.
It's a promise that no distance will ever
　　put space between two hearts... the
　　hearts of true friends.
Yes, our friendship is a promise — a promise
　　of support and laughter and hope. A
　　promise of loyalty and love and caring
　　that will grow stronger with each day.
Our friendship is a promise... that will last
　　a lifetime.

—————————
Donna Gephart

We'll Always Be There
for Each Other

There is no greater feeling
Than knowing that someone
Is truly there for you.

It is a comfort beyond measure
To know that you can trust
Your life and your heart
To someone who forever understands.
To have someone who always
Makes you feel better with just
The right words
Offers solace beyond compare.

To be uplifted in such an effortless way
That you almost come to expect it
Is a rarity to be treasured.

For this I give
My heartfelt thanks
And my love to you,
Dear Friend,
Now and always.
Thank you for the joy
That you bring to
My world every day.

— Lynn Barnhart

To a Friend
Who Is like
an Angel to Me

In this life, on this earth, and in the days that I spend trying to do the best I can, I know that I wouldn't be half the person I am if it weren't for a little divine inspiration that comes from having a friend like you.

You have been my saving grace on more occasions than you will ever know. You are my friend, my see-me-through and inspire-my-smile companion. When you listen, you hear what I'm really trying to say. And when you communicate, your words come straight from the heart.

You make me feel that "yes, my presence really does matter!" You constantly add to my joys and to the value of my self-worth, and I wish I could thank you every day.

You are so amazing. Compared to you, I feel like I'll always be in training for my own set of wings. You are my very own down-to-earth angel. I cherish you very much, and I want to thank you, my dear friend, for the way you bring so much joy to my life.

Marin McKay

I'm so lucky to have a friend like you

One of the best feelings
in the whole world
comes from being a friend...
and having a friend in return.

I wouldn't trade my friendship with
you for anything... because I know that
nothing else could ever begin to bring me
the contentment, the wonderful
craziness, the support and the caring,
the laughter, the understanding, and
all the thousands of things that we
share together...

One of the sweetest feelings
in the whole world
comes from knowing that
everything we share — and the joy
that graces our lives — will warm our
hearts forever, in all the days ahead.

For no matter how far apart
our paths may wander,
and no matter how long it's been,
it's so great to know that...

you and I will always be
the closest and
dearest of friends.

———————

Lorrie Westfall

May You Always Know How Much I Care

A long time ago we built something between us that is still so strong, so special, and so lasting. I feel connected to you in ways that are hard to explain, yet they are filled with meaning and they speak to my soul.

I am so glad God brought you my way — directing your path into my life and giving me a friend to share with and care about.

Today, stop for a moment and let the memories we have made hold your heart — and please know how very much I care. You are very important to me, and you always will be.

I want you to know that no matter where your life takes you, you will always have a place in my heart.

— Denise Johnston

My Friend, You Are a Gift to the World

Your friendship is priceless,
your caring is my treasure,
and your smile is all it takes
to brighten each day.
Your kindness is my comfort,
your friendship is a wonderful gift,
and your laughter is light
for each day's journey.
Knowing someone like you
is like having a rainbow on my doorstep
every season of the year.
You add color to the dullest days
and beauty to my dreams;
you help me search for all
    the treasures I hope to find.
Today, may your heart smile
knowing how much you are loved.
May every day bring you
all the wonderful discoveries
    you deserve,
just to remind you
what a wonderful gift you are
    to the world.

— Linda E. Knight

ACKNOWLEDGMENTS

We gratefully acknowledge the permission granted by the following authors, publishers, and authors' representatives to reprint poems or excerpts from their publications.

PrimaDonna Entertainment Corp. for "My Definition of a Good Friend Is You" by Donna Fargo. Copyright © 2002 by PrimaDonna Entertainment Corp. All rights reserved.

debbie burton-peddle for "The First Time I Met You, I Knew We Would Be Friends." Copyright © 2003 by debbie burton-peddle. All rights reserved.

Autumn Banks for "You've Planted Some Beautiful Seeds in the Garden of My Life." Copyright © 2003 by Autumn Banks. All rights reserved.

Kathy Larson for "The Friendship Wish." Copyright © 2003 by Kathy Larson. All rights reserved.

Carrie Cramer for "You and I Are Bigger than Any of Our Differences." Copyright © 2003 by Carrie Cramer. All rights reserved.

Vickie M. Worsham for "Old Friends Are the Best Gifts in Life." Copyright © 2003 by Vickie M. Worsham. All rights reserved.

Dallas Woodburn for "We Go Together Like...." Copyright © 2003 by Dallas Woodburn. All rights reserved.

Jason Blume for "You've Made a Difference in My Life." Copyright © 2003 by Jason Blume. All rights reserved.

Barbara J. Hall for "A Best Friend... Is What You'll Always Be to Me." Copyright © 2003 by Barbara J. Hall. All rights reserved.

Barbara Cage for "Friends Are the Heartstrings of Life." Copyright © 2003 by Barbara Cage. All rights reserved.

Donna Gephart for "Our Friendship Is a Promise." Copyright © 2003 by Donna Gephart. All rights reserved.

A careful effort has been made to trace the ownership of selections used in this anthology in order to obtain permission to reprint copyrighted material and give proper credit to the copyright owners. If any error or omission has occurred, it is completely inadvertent, and we would like to make corrections in future editions provided that written notification is made to the publisher:

SPS STUDIOS, INC., P.O. Box 4549, Boulder, Colorado 80306.

*One of the sweetest feelings
in the whole world
comes from knowing that
everything we share   and the joy
that graces our lives   will warm our
hearts forever, in all the days ahead.*

Lorrie Westfall

When you have a good friend, you possess a treasure that only a fortunate few ever find. Like the brightest star in the night sky, their friendship outshines all the rest. This is the person you rely on when no one else understands what you're going through. You share all the best times and make so many wonderful memories. No matter where you go in life or how often you see each other, this friend will always hold that place in your soul where the greatest people in your life are remembered forever.

At the heart of this book is an acknowledgment of friendship's power to entwine two destinies together in a supportive, encouraging relationship. Friendship makes two people the best they can be — for themselves and each other — as they go through life together.

Blue Mountain Arts®
Boulder, Colorado

$10.95 U.S. $14.94 Canada
ISBN 0-88396-770-7

51095

9 780883 967706

W9-CEP-017